AF304801

Igor Terentiev
Tenderness Record
The Life of Ilya Zdanevich

bie ᵇᵃᵒ series   militant zaum investigations volume 3

Introduction

Igor Terentiev's *Tenderness Record: The Life of Ilya Zdanevich* was published in August 1919 in Tbilisi by the imprint of 41°.[1] Terentiev, the "theoretician and a militant polemicist of zaum"[2] had arrived in Tbilisi in 1918, where he joined in the activities of the Futurist Syndicate, a group of poets and painters including Alexei Kruchenykh, brothers Ilya and Kirill Zdanevich, Lado Gudiashvili, and others.[3] On January 19th 1918, the Futurist Syndicate organised an evening of zaum poetry where, in addition to readings from members of the group, Georg von Charasoff gave a lecture interpreting zaum with psychoanalytic concepts.[4] Charasoff further developed his approach with another lecture on 'Freud's Theories and Zaum Poetry' on April 5th 1918, also as a part of the programme organised by the Futurist Syndicate.[5] In this exceptional milieu, Terentiev who had been up until then a visual artist, discovered zaum and Freud, and joined a collective of artists busy with publishing.[6]

In April 1918, a pamphlet authored jointly by Kruchenykh and Terentiev appeared under the title 'A Conversation about *Malacholy In a Bathrobe*', which was the first symptomatic reading of zaum poetry. A large part of this reading, of Kruchneykh's own poetry book *Malakholia v Kapote* [Malacholy In a Bathrobe], was about sexuality.[7] Apart from the subterranean fields of zaum, they were also investigating the intimate dynamics of language.[8] On one occasion,

Terentiev described himself as a "deepener of the erotics of Russian language (anal)."[9]

Terentiev published five books in 1919 in Tbilisi – *Kruchenykh Grandiozar* [Kruchenykh, the Grandiose], *Heruvimy Svistjat* [The Cherubim Whistle], *17 Erundovykh Orudie* [17 Nonsensical Tools], *Fakt* [Fact], and *Rekord Nezhnosti* [Tenderness Record]. He published one further book in Tbilisi in 1920, *Traktat o Sploshnom Neprilichi* [Treatise on Total Obscenity], until his next and the final book, *John Reed*, which appeared in 1927, in Leningrad.[10]

Alexander Brener once wrote that Terentiev's "case is exceptional," as he challenged "the framework set by the intellectual cultural paradigm in Russia," always aspiring towards the unity of "culture and the state."[11] Perhaps this is the reason why, for a long period of time, he was disbanded both by the intellectual culture and the official state. Vladimir Markov, an eminent historian of Russian Futurism, writes that "it is not known what happened to Terentiev after 1928."[12] Now, thanks to a series of publications dedicated to the life and work of Terentiev, we have a clearer picture of his work in the twenties, as well as the humiliations in forced labour camps he experienced in the thirties, and of his murder in the Stalinist purges of 1937.[13]

The first reprint of *Tenderness Record*, together with most of Terentiev's other writings were published in *Sobraniye Sochineniy* [Collected Works] in Bologna in 1988.[14] It was later reprinted in the collection of Ilya Zdanevich's Futurist writings.[15]

                    Introduction

The French translation was published in a beautifully designed edition by Clemens Hiver in Paris in 1990.[16]

In *Tenderness Record*, Terentiev "reveals the plot of Zdanevich's zaum dra[ma]s, comparing them with the vertep theatre."[17] This was a difficult task because Zdanevich wrote his dras using words "in transcription as they were heard, deliberately ignoring the rules of Russian spelling," which made his zaum writings "difficult to read." Despite all these difficulties, as Tatyana Nikolskaya claims, "Terentiev managed to isolate the skeleton of a plot in the dra."[18]

In his biography, Terentiev portrayed Zdanevich as a product of the general intellect, or more precisely, his artistic genius is portrayed as a product of collective creativity. With Terentiev, Zdanevich's early concept of *Vsechestvo* [Everythingism], referring to "the synthesis of all artistic and literary forms," had become plagiarism, in today's language, corresponding to some kind of poetic commoning. The ubiquitous link was made to include all schools of poetic expression, and everything was amalgamated into zaum. The freedom of appropriation was boldly stated by Terentiev in the conclusion of *17 Nonsensical Tools*: "Down with the Authors! We need to use the words of others, legalise plagiarism."[19] Kruchenykh also utilised this commoning practice, when in his *Ozhireny Roz* [The Flattening of Roses], he used Terentiev's poems to present his own discoveries.[20] But it was Terentiev who gave the ultimate theoretical expression to this practice with his "route of sphericity" or "global itinerary" [*marshrut sharizny*], which proposed that poetic words would circle around the globe until they reach their destination, open to contaminating influences as they crossed strange and exotic languages.[21]

In this volume we are also publishing a letter by Terentiev sent to Zdanevich on February 5th 1924, when he was heading the short-lived Phonological Department at the State Institute of Artistic Culture, or GINKhUK [Gosudarstvennyi institut khudozhestvennoi kultury], directed by Kazimir Malevich. Terentiev's programme at the Department was to "translate" Marx into zaum, and to establish a scientific base for the sonority of voice experiments.[22] The letter to Zdanevich is less explicit about the Marxist undertones of the project, but is unambiguous with regards to the methodological implications of zaum – recounting the intent to compose a new type of encyclopaedia and glossary based on this logic. He attached to this short letter a very short zaum play titled *Iordano Bruno*, a play Terentiev never shared with anyone but Zdanevich.[23]

Terentiev's zaum is "characterised by brevity, variety, and flexibility,"[24] which in *Iordano Bruno* manifested itself as an accelerated and condensed "global itinerary." It condensed the thesis that "zaum is crucial for the creation of linguistic internationalism,"[25] and "is the primordial form of poetry,"[26] introducing 'humanity' as one of the actors and the 'heretic' as the hero of the play. Resembling Zdanevich's vertep-style dras, the plot of the play is very simple: Giordano Bruno sits and works in

Introduction

the Place de la Concorde. Schmetterlink and his wife Kolumbia stroll by after dinner, they see Bruno. Kolumbia reports this to the Pope. Her husband condemns her and gathers some people to listen to Bruno's wisdom. The entirety of the human race assembles. Police also appear. Kolumbia arrives with a papal order to burn Bruno at the stake, which the police then do. The people leave and the two men are left alone, Bruno remains quite alive. Schmetterlink condemns the people for their frivolity. A girl runs in and Schmetterlink wants to kill her. Kolumbia saves her. The Mona Lisa appears, and asks "What's the matter, little girl?" The girl responds with a string of vowels: "u o a e i e a o u y i i i."[27]

Like many zaum plays, this one about heresy is also "difficult to read," but pronouncing it aloud could give a "physiological joy,"[28] which is what we deem the world of Terentiev and Zdanevich to be very much about. We hope this thin volume of Terentiev, the first of its kind in the English language, will give an impression of that guttural flavour.

1 The cover of the first edition of *Tenderness Record* book has a huge letter ю [yu] overprinted on the title. The inner cover reads: *rekord nezhnosti –zhitiye il'ia zdanevicha pisal yego drug terent'yev kartinki yego brata kirilla* [Tenderness Record – the life of Ilya Zdanevich written by his friend Igor Terentiev, with drawings by his brother Kirill]. The book was designed by Ilya Zdanevich, and was printed by the Printing House of the Union of Cities of the Republic of Georgia in 1919. There are ten illustrations by Kirill Zdanevich printed with blue ink. The size of the book is 15 × 13.5 cm, with twenty-four pages. There is no information about the print run of the book. Before appearing as a book, 'Tenderness Record' was published as an article in the only issue of *41°: yezhenedel'naya gazeta* [weekly newspaper], no. 1, Tbilisi, July 14–20, 1919, p. 3.

2 Vladimir Markov, *Russian Futurism: A History*, University of California Press, 1968, p. 358.

3 The Futurist Syndicate was founded in November 1917 by Kruchenykh, the Zdanevich brothers, Nikolay Chernyavsky, Lado Gudiashvili, Kara Darvish and Zygmunt Waliszewski. Tatyana Nikolskaya, 'Sindikat Futurista', *Pojmovnik Ruske Avangarde Vol. 3*, Grafički Zavod Hrvatske, Zagreb, 1985, pp. 145–154.

4 Nikolskaya, 'Sindikat Futurista', p. 150.

5 Gerald Janecek, *Zaum: The Transrational Poetry of Russian Futurism*, San Diego State University Press, 1996, p. 254. Georg von Charasoff (Georgy Kharazov, 1877–1931) was a Marxist scholar of economics originally from Tbilisi, who returned to his home country from Zurich during the War, and joined local avant-garde artists. From 1918 to 1921, when he introduced Freudian theories to the Futurists, he was a professor of mathematics at the Polytechnic University in Tbilisi. Both Kruchenykh and Terentiev's interest in Freud and psychoanalysis was roused by Charasoff's lectures and articles. For an excellent overview of Charasoff's turbulent intellectual biography, including his time in Tbilisi, Baku and Ukraine, one should read Christian Gehrke, 'Georg von Charasoff: A Neglected Contributor to the Classical-Marxian Tradition', *History of Economics Review, 62:1*, 2015, pp. 1–37.

6 Tatyana Nikolskaya, *'Fantasticheskiy gorod' Russkaya kulturnaya zhizn' v Tbilisi, 1917–1921* ['Fantasy City': Russian Cultural Life in Tbilisi, 1917–1921], Pyataya Strana, Moscow, 2000, pp. 57–133.

Introduction

7 Igor Terentiev and Alexei Kruchenykh, 'Conversation about Malacholy In a Bathrobe', *Experiment, No. 1*, 1995, pp. 284–288. In this conversation Kruchenykh has some interesting remarks about Zdanevich's *Yanko, King of Albania*. Walter Comins-Richmond, 'Igor Terentiev and Alexei Kruchenykh', *Experiment No. 1*, 1995, pp. 281–284. *Malakholia v Kapote* [Malacholy In a Bathrobe] was published in 1918 in Tbilisi.

8 "Poetry as an exercise for the voice, as material for linguistics, as a potential source for new words, and for fertilisation of language (in zaum, sound rots and thought sprouts)." Igor Terentiev, *17 Erundovykh Orudii* [17 Nonsensical Tools, 1919], quoted in Vladimir Markov, *Russian Futurism*, p. 359.

9 Quoted from Tatyana Nikolskaya, 'Igor Terentiev/ Zaum', *Pojmovnik Ruske Avangarde, Vol. 3*, 1985, p. 217. The same essay, given as a talk in Zagreb, is published in Russian as 'I. Terentiev', *Russian Literature, Vol. XXII*, 1987, p. 80. Terentiev's quote is taken from the dedication written on the copy of the book owned privately by the author of the article. Gerald Janecek claims that the article was written by Sergei Sigov, and mistakenly attributed to Nikolskaya. Janecek, *Zaum*, p. 398.

10 Terentiev wrote the play *John Reed*, based on the book by John Reed, *Ten Days that Shook the World*, the classic account on the October Revolution. The second edition was published as *Dzhon Rid: P'yesa v chetyrokh deystviyakh* [John Reed: A Play in Four Acts], Moscow-Leningrad, 1927.

11 Alexander Brener, 'Intelligentskaya Kultura i Precedent Terent'yeva' [Intellectual Culture and the Precedent of Terentiev], *Terentievsky Sbornik,* edited by Sergey Kudriavtsev, Hylea, Moscow, 1996, pp. 13–18.

12 Markov, *Russian Futurism*, p. 358, 362.

13 The first comprehensive anthology on Terentiev's work was *Igor Terentiev, Sobraniye Sochineniy* [Collected Works], Eurasiatica: Quaderni del Dipartmento di Studi Eurasiatici Universita degli Studi di Venezia, edited by Marzio Marzaduri and Tatyana Nikolskaya, S. Francesco Publishers, Bologna, 1988. Apart from Marazaduri and Nikolskaya's introductions, the book is generously contextualised with extensive annotations. It also includes a large collection of contemporary reviews of Terentiev, mostly covering his theatrical work. *Igor Terentiev, Moi pokhorony: Stikhi. Pis'ma. Sledstvennyye pokazaniya.*

           Introduction

Dokumenty [My funeral: Poems. Letters. Investigative testimony. The documents], Hylea, Moscow, 1993. In this slim volume there are valuable documents about Terentiev's arrests and interrogations in the thirties. Two volumes of *Terentievsky Sbornik* [Terentiev Collection], published in 1996 and 1998, edited by Sergey Kudriavtsev, Hylea, Moscow. Apart from articles by and about Terentiev, these collections also include contributions on other avant-garde writers associated with zaum. *Dva tipograficheskikh shedevra. Faksimil'noye izdaniye. Stat'i. Kommentarii* [Two typographic masterpieces. Facsimile edition. Articles. Comments], edited by Andrey Rossomakhin, European University Press, St. Petersburg, 2014. This volume is a reprint of *17 Erundovykh Orudie* and *Traktat o Sploshnom Neprilichi* with commentaries and extensive annotations.

14 Igor Terentiev, *Sobraniye Sochineniy* [Collected Works], pp. 237–260. Includes facsimile reprint of *Rekord Nezhnosti*, with Kirill Zdanevich's drawings.

15 Reprinted without Kirill's drawings in Ilya Zdanevich, *Filosofiya futurista: Romany i zaumnyye dramy*, Hylea, 2008, pp. 708–711.

16 Igor Terentiev, *Un Record de Tendresse : hagiographie d'Ilia Zdanevitch*, translated by Régis Geyraud, Clemens Hiver, Paris, 1990.

17 Nikolskaya, 'Igor Terentiev v Tiflise', p. 197. Vertep is a simplified puppet theatre and drama, popular in Russian and Ukrainian folk culture.

18 Tatyana Nikolskaya, 'Russian Writers in Georgia in 1917–1921', *The Ardis Anthology of Russian Futurism*, edited by Ellendea and Carl Proffer, Ardis, Michigan, 1980, p. 303.

19 Igor Terentiev, *7 Erundovykh Orudie*, Tbilisi, 1919, p. 12, quoted from Terentiev, *Sobraniye Sochineniy*, p. 179. Terentiev's practice of appropriating other poets' corpus is meticulously discussed in Vera Faber, 'Iskusstvo vo vtoroy stepeni. K voprosu intertekstual'nogo prisutstviya Il'ya Zdanevicha i Alekseya Kruchenykh v tvorchestve Igorya Terentyeva' [Art in the second degree. On the question of the intertextual presence of Ilya Zdanevich and Alexei Kruchenykh in the work of Igor Terentiev], *Dada po-russki*, edited by Kornelija Ičin, Belgrade University, 2013, pp. 171–188.

20 One of them titled 'To the Occupation of Palestine by the British', deserves full quotation:
 Soyneka zhyneyra
 Lipitaroza kuba
 Veyda leyde
 Tsyube
 Tuka stuka vey
 Oyok kyok Eb'
 Kheptsup
 Up
 Pi
Quoted from Janecek, *Zaum*, p. 258. Reprinted in Terentiev, *Sobraniye Sochineniy*, p. 154.

21 In his lectures in Paris, Zdanevich used this concept to argue for the internationalism of zaum.

22 'Terentiev's letter to Kruchenykh, December 23rd 1923', in Terentiev, *Sobraniye Sochineniy*, p. 400.

23 Sergey Sigov, 'O teatre russkikh futuristiv', 1988, quoted in Janecek, Zaum, p. 273. Terentiev's letter to Zdanevich, including the play *Iordano Bruno*, sent from Leningrad to Paris on February 5th 1924 was first published in *L'avanguardia a Tiflis* in its original Russian with an introduction written by Giovanna Pagani Cesa, 'Une Lettera di Igor Terent'ev a Il'ja Zdanevič', *L'Avanguardia a Tiflis*, Quaderni del Seminario di Iranistica, Uralo-Altaistica e Caucasologia dell' Università degli Studi di Venezia, edited by L. Magarotto, M. Marzaduri, and G. P. Cesa, Venice, 1982, pp. 269–280.

24 Janecek, *Zaum*, p. 271.

25 Igor Terentiev, 'Kto Lef, Kto Praf' [Whose Left, Whose Right, 1924], *Sobraniye Sochineniy*, p. 288.

26 Alexei Kruchenykh, 'Declaration of Zaum Language' [Deklaratsiia zaumnogo iazyka, 1921], *Russian Futurism Through its Manifestos, 1912–1928*, edited by Anna Lawton, Cornell University Press, 1988, p. 182.

27 Janecek, *Zaum*, pp. 271–273. In an alternative ending, which is not included in *L'Avanguardia a Tiflis* and *Sobraniye Sochineniy*, after the girl's response, there is a slow installation of the letter 'Y', followed by the liturgical singing at the end. Our translation is from the version, which was published in *Vot tragediya Jordano Bruno: v nabore i v avtorskoy rukopisi – pis'me Il'ye Zdanevichu* [Here is the tragedy of Iordano Bruno: in typesetting and as the author's manuscript – a letter to Ilya Zdanevich], edited by Sergey Kudriavtsev, Hylea, Moscow, 2000. The version can be found online, read by Igor Loshchilov.

28 Boris Konstriktor, 'Slovo i Telo. O spektaklyakh 'Teatralnoy laboratori' [Word and Body. About the performances of 'The Theatre Laboratory']', *Isskusstvo Leningrada, No. 10*, 1990, p. 29. Konstriktor reviewed the first performance of *Iordano Bruno*

  Introduction

in the Theatre Museum on June
6th 1988 under the direction
of V. Maksimov. Konstriktor,
himself an avant-garde writer,
criticised the performance
as failing to express the
"physiological" dimension
of zaum. Konstriktor also
wrote a long 'deconstruction'
of *Iordano Bruno*, published
in the mid-nineties. Boris
Konstriktor, 'Tragediya Igorya
Terent'yeva Jordano Bruno:
opyt strukturnogo preskaza'
[The Tragedy of Igor Terentiev
Iordano Bruno: experiment of
structural retelling], *Terentievsky
Sbornik 1996*, pp. 64–78.

Introduction

TENDERNESS RECORD
the life of ilya zdanevich
written by his friend
igor terentiev

41º

with
drawings
by his brother
kirill zdanevich

The poet's early years, his childhood, are of nobody's concern. All that is known is that he was exceptionally handsome at the time. In his teens, he graduated from the Tbilisi Gymnasium, then as a young man from the Faculty of Law at St. Petersburg University, and came of age somewhere between the Caucasus, St. Petersburg, Moscow and Paris, where he would make appearances with public lectures, recitations of other people's poetry and so on.

Mutual acquaintances share anecdotes about the "School of Kisses" allegedly established by Ilya somewhere up North, and talk about his brilliant speech in Kislovodsk, carousing, lechery, impudence and the jovial nature of this kind-hearted, egotistic, wry, sentimental, reserved, hot-headed and criminal young man.

Inspiring in people not only respect, contempt and anger, but also participation, Ilya would hear a great deal of useful advice from relatives and friends, who always felt that the youth was destined for great heights.

The young man listened to everyone and heeded every bit of their advice, allotting a week, a month, or a year to each. At the same time, with nobody's appreciation — of his own kind nature alone — Ilya became a poet. This happened a long time ago, and was discovered last year, when in Tbilisi there leapt up an orange flea — the poet's first book, "Yanko, King of Albania."[1]

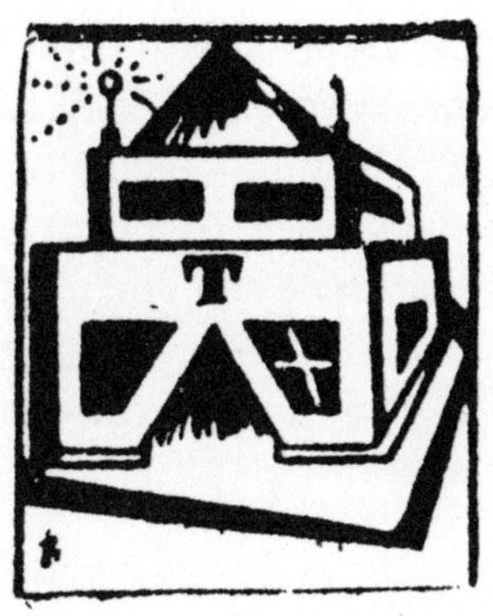

41º theatre

Tenderness Record

A cinematographic shot of all sounds Ilya had heard or would like to have heard over the course of more than 20 years!

An overture to the poet's further plays that have been released since, or are in print at this time.

All of humanity's ills have been strung to a near breaking point in "Yanko".

Acquisitiveness — Yanko catches the loathed flea and writes "*propeti* of Yanko" on it. Beggardom
and lack
of gender —
"*Yanko yt clothed in trausrs of sam wans sholdr shood in nju tajms*"
["*Yanko clothed it in trousers off someone's shoulder, shoed in new times*"]
Cowardice — "*popsi momsi,*"
"*ana vanja*

                                        dublja,"

stupidity
and pride — "*ae bie bae bie bao biu baæ.*"

Tenderness Record

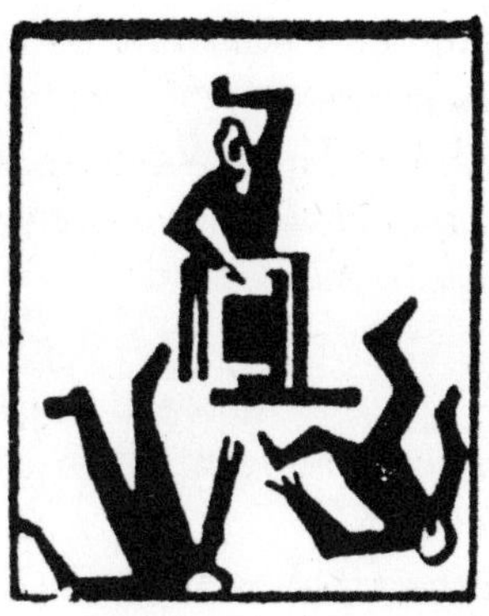

kislovodsk speech

Tenderness Record

The plot is simple enough: vagabond Yanko encounters some bandits in the middle of a quarrel. As someone entirely alien and impersonal, Yanko is coerced into kinghood. He is fearful. He is glued to the throne with syndeticon,[2] tries to unstick, is helped by an Austrian named Yrental: they both shout "*wota*," but there is no water, and Yanko dies by the knife of the bandits, letting out a "*foof.*" That is all. A story worthy of a nativity or a puppet show.

Here we observe Russia in the 19th century.

Gatchina, oak cupboard and Seraphim of Sarov.[3]

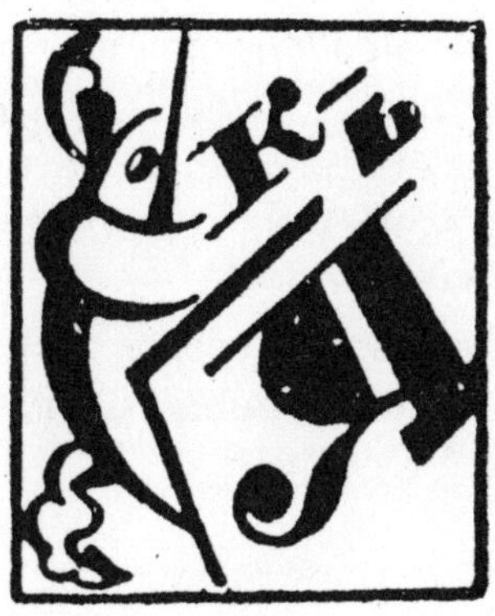

orange flea

Tenderness Record

Ilya Zdanevich's voice is heard in "Yanko" well enough, using the letter "y" as the root to easily reach the upper-register "j" —

"*albejnjen lengweg livs alongsaid rushn stems from yt*"

[*"Albanian language lives alongside, Russian stems from it"*]

"yts language" uncovers all intrinsically Russian capabilities, which however have not been used in "Yanko" — there is not a single woman in it, not a single "yi" — not a drop of moisture.[4]

The unbelievable drought of the lexical texture, the coarse paper, the front cover's colour of petrified bile — have made many take Ilya Zdanevich for an academic and a bureaucrat.

The poet has shared the fate of his protagonist: lack of "water!," 41 degrees!

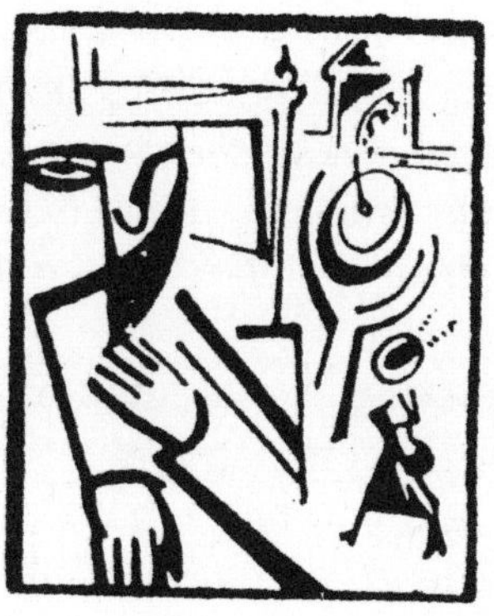

gatchina, oak cupboard and seraphim of sarov

Tenderness Record

Crisp nose! Zdanevich seeks a soulful softness (slobber of love): the wellspring of a drive towards anal eroticism! Contracts abdominal typhoid! Writes a new drama "Donkey for Rent" — a compress of woman piously applied with abandon, to fiancé "A" here, "B" there, and, simply by mistake, an ass elsewhere.[5]

All obscenely love-filled words: eel, ooze, woo, ess in wanton jubilation, outsalivating even the slobberiest of poets, Velimir Khlebnikov himself:

splttley,   pOking
isalisAlivate   inUndies   qWlmmly
hUmptydumpty
isllp shAftous
pEck
iffOOfssy fLOwring unAbi lUf
gyaenEEy   talEstis
mavzEpit   nettlb   rOckarock
gApey gOOpy Elfy
gArters

Tenderness Record

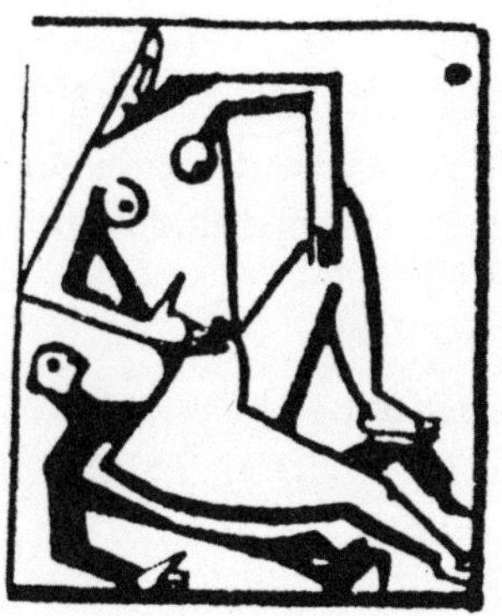

compress of woman

 Tenderness Record

bIllygoat
stIcky frIlls pUff
mEdic mUte sqUElsquelch hOlde alumInii
Ikcufkcuf   cOOc   sqUIsh   iyOU Eff
trIckling ypfYAk
IAnguey   drAw   tEEtly   mmE
heahEAdy

.   .   .   .

A tenderness record has been set by Ilya
Zdanevich, brimming with delight!

.   .   .   .

.   .   .   .

    The third drama of the "dunkeeness" cycle
features a more committed transformation
of human into donkey: the host speaks of the
"Eastr Ailand" characters with near affection:
"Merchant a veritable ass crætor more so two
and a half stone broads also tripe."[6]

                    Tenderness Record

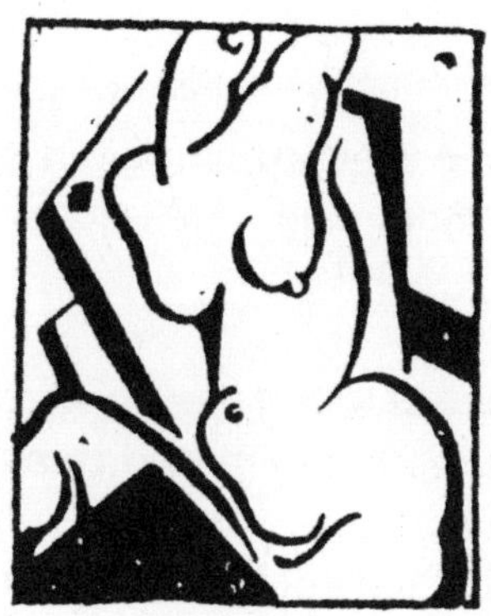

tenderness record

Tenderness Record

Quite the joyful drama: everybody dies and everybody resurrects — period ... monthly!

Two and a ½ broads (character reference) — first — earth-dusted mother; old crone's makeup. Second — sister-in-law with hysteria in a bathroom.

The half — a complete æ![7]

And the crætor's kindest words are dedicated to the half:

"meadowy
laidown spanker
doey."

This is nightingale's trill (the letters ch, sh, sch', ts, s, f, kh, z — convey feelings of the flesh: scratch, caress, fondle, tickle...)

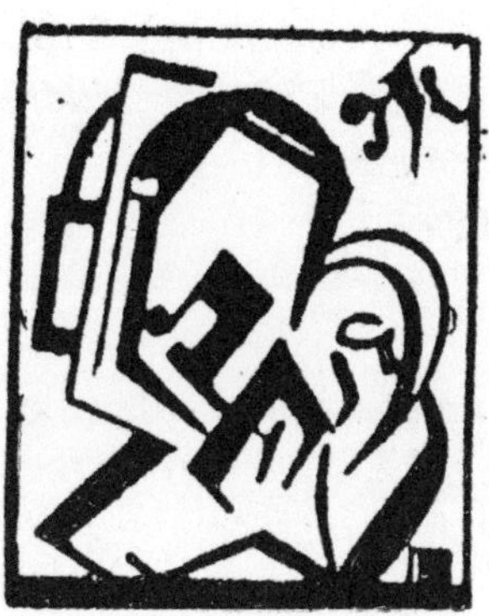

meadowy, laidown spanker

Tenderness Record

The half's voice is the simplest one in the broad orchestra:

KON with superimposed UKIT / KONII / K   i.e.   KUKIT KONII KONK

She also adores sibilant sounds: *chya, bzypyzy*!

The Ibsenesque irresoluteness notable in "Donkey for Rent" has disappeared in "Eastr Ailand": here the "unclovenhoofed hopes" come true: easter negative indicator of death menstruation of stone broads resolve act easter and crætor

> *sprinkles crætor with broad blood*
> *crætor*
> *alives runs*
> *houst*

Fino.

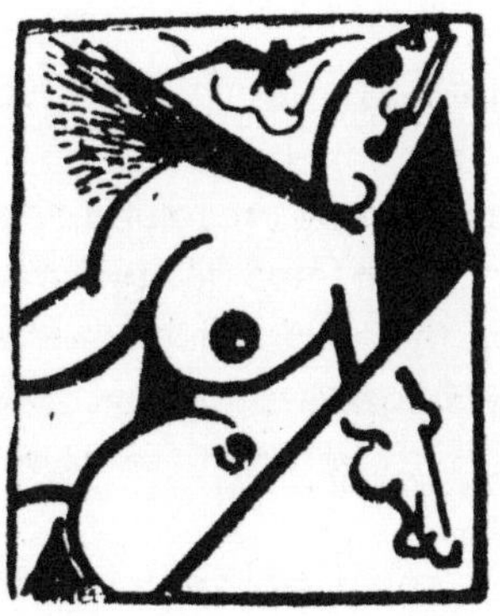

the half a complete œ

Tenderness Record

A smart person never objects to merit.

Ilya Zdanevich an angel of compact stature and an insolent singer.

For the next séance: "Zga Yakaby" and "lidantyu faram."[8] A place for the 2nd part of the "Life of Ilya Zdanevich."

To the end!

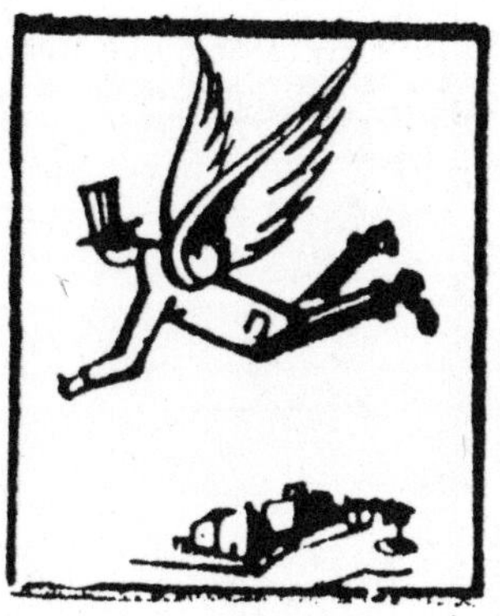

angel of compact stature

 Tenderness Record

TO ILYA ZDANEVICH
TeaR maRchinG
tO blAde tiP
cobrA nose GoGGiG
thullA expRessiNg
eliAh lla A A A
ABycYDyEfgHYI
JKL !
ZdA !!
NeViCH !!!
I L Y A !!!

Tenderness Record

to the end

Tenderness Record

1 *Yanko, Krul Albanskaya* [Yanko, King of Albania] was published, with an orange cover, in May 1918 in Tbilisi by the Sindikat Futuristov [Futurist Syndicate], a short lived avant-garde platform initiated by Zdanevich.

2 An obsolete brand of gelatine-based liquid adhesive used in the end of 19th and at the beginning of 20th centuries.

3 The town of Gatchina lies near St. Petersburg. The Great Gatchina Palace was one of the main residences of the Russian Imperial Family during the 18th and 19th centuries. Seraphim of Sarov (1754–1833, born Prókhor Isídorovich Moshnin) is one of the most renowned Russian Saints and is venerated in the Eastern Orthodox Church.

4 Zdanevich wrote in *Iliazda* that Terentiev was mistaken – "there is a woman, but she is a flea." Ilya Zdanevich, *Iliazda at the Birthday Party* (bie-bao vol 2), p. 44.

5 Ilya Zdanevich's *Donkey for Rent* was a second volume in the '*dunkeeness*' series, and was published in the anthology *Sofii Georgievne Melynikovoi. Fantasticheskii Kabachek. Tiflis 1917-1918-1919* [The Sofia Georgievna Melnikova. The Fantastic Tavern. Tiflis 1917-1918-1919], edited by Igor Terentiev, et al., 41°, Tbilisi, 1919, pp. 39–68.

6 Ilya Zdanevich, *Easter Ailand*, 41°, Tbilisi, 1919. A thirty-two page booklet printed by the Printing House of the Union of Cities of the Republic of Georgia.

7 Refers to letter ѣ [ye, yat] used in old Russian orthography. As мѣсячный [mesyachniy, monthly].

8 Ilya Zdanevich, *Zga Yakaby*, 41°, Tbilisi, 1920. Forty-four pages, printed by the Printing House of the Union of Cities of the Republic of Georgia.
Ilya Zdanevich - Iliazd, *lidantYu faram* [Ledentu as Beacon], 41°, Paris, 1923. Sixty-one pages, printed in the l'Imprimerie Union.

Tenderness Record

A
Note on a
Letter from
Igor Terentiev
to Ilya Zdanevich[1]

Giovanna Pagani Cesa

In the Zdanevich Archive in Paris, kindly made available to us by Hélène Zdanevich, there are five letters from Igor Terentiev, all but one sent between 1920 and 1924 and all addressed to his friend Ilya. To varying degrees they shed light on individual moments in the life and activity of the versatile, whimsical theorist of the 41°, who suddenly appeared in the Georgian sky of the Russian avant-garde to disappear into thin air only a few years later, leaving behind few texts, meagre biographical information and many unverifiable rumours.

Terentiev left Tbilisi for Moscow in 1922 and remained there for two years. It was from here he wrote the fourth letter, dated May 4th 1923.[2] The final and undoubtedly most interesting letter dated February 5th 1924, which we publish here, clarifies the strained relations between Kruchenykh and Terentiev as representative figures of the abstract, alogical, fundamentally anarchist and antisocial line of the Russian avant-garde on one side, and on the other side of the Futurists of the Lef [Left Front of the Arts], now immersed in the ideology of productivism. Kruchenykh and Terentiev, both also representatives of 41°, were attempting to form an opposition which, in today's political language, we could define as 'entryism'. Kruchenykh, however, faced with the tendency within the Lef to connect zaum to the specific needs of the new society, as "its immediate and conscious instrument,"[3] was willing to compromise with the left front of arts; while Terentiev, ever faithful to the ideas and spirit of the

A Note on a Letter

41^0, comes to consider the Lef as an opportunistic and unfaithful usurper of the radical avant-garde, by attempting to reverse the situation, completely unrealistically, and to absorb Mayakovsky's group within a new enlarged platform of 41^0. We reproduce in full the passage of the letter relating to this situation:

> "The ideological front has been proclaimed in art. The journal *Lef*, under the direction of Mayakovsky, aims to unify the Left Front of the Arts.
>
> All those who are not in the Lef are unbearable scoundrels. But the Lef itself isn't much better.
>
> The position must be socially clear; for this reason in Lef, Krucenykh and I occupied the cot [*la branda*] on the extreme left, hung the file from 41^0 by the bedside and declared ourselves sick.
>
> One can point to the poetic international only through zaum. Between Futurism, so to speak, and the Russian Revolution, there is the sign of equality. But the revolution on an international scale = 41^0... Thus, for example, Ilya Zdanevich lives in Paris, Kruchenykh is a depraved Tatar, Terentiev is Georgian, Turkish, etc. the mixing of languages on the basis of zaum.
> This is theory:
> and it is *enough*!

A Note on a Letter

In practice: 1) one way or another we have to
publish; 2) your dramas and plays have to be
staged in Moscow theatres by us; 3) I advise
you to publish in Paris even just one issue of
Lef in French. It will come out as it is the 41^0.
The method is proven and it is the only one: the
usurpation of what has always been ours! Isn't
the name Lef ours anyway? And with them this
will be casually and uselessly lost."[4]

Terentiev's attempt to influence the ideas of the Lef
from within was, of course, doomed to failure. His
collaboration with the journal is reduced to the poem
'1-oe Maya' [The First of May], published alongside
a poem by Kruchenykh of the same title, a short
reportage essay 'The Transcaucasian LEF' (The
Company of the 41°)[5] and a controversial open letter
written in response to an article by Lev Sosnovsky that
appeared in *Pravda*, which insinuated certain doubts
about the political past of the members of the 41^0.[6]

In June 1924, embittered by Kruchenykh's
unclear and contradictory position which seemed to
him as "bewitched by Lef" and as being reluctant to
support the 41°, Terentiev left Moscow and moved
to Leningrad.[7] Here, with unwavering enthusiasm,
an absolute lack of a sense of reality and by this
point an anachronistic loyalty [*ormai anacronistica
coerenza*], he continued circulating the ideas of the
41^0. As we read in his final letter, in just five months
he had held "fourteen to seventeen conferences"
with poetry readings, presenting Zdanevich's Parisian

     A Note on a Letter

activities; had organised a group of young people under the banner of 41° and was preparing to publish various materials. At the GINKhUK [*Gosudarstvennyi institut khudozhestvennoi kultury,* the State Institute of Artistic Culture], he worked together with Kazimir Malevich and Aleksandr Tufanov[8] to establish a "phonological department" with its own scientific bulletin. Under the platform of "non-objectivity," he was planning to unite various sections of the Institute in a federation which would be represented by 41° for literature and poetry, and by Malevich's Suprematism and Matyushin's Zorved for the visual art.

Though most of these projects and intentions remain, once again, only on paper, the Leningrad years nonetheless mark a happy creative moment for Terentiev in the field of theatre production. It is not known exactly when he started working as a theatre director, perhaps in Tbilisi, or even in Moscow, before arriving in Georgia,[9] but during his stay in Leningrad Terentiev staged a series of successful theatrical projects up until 1927 when his work *Revizor,* alongside Meyerhold's activities were criticised as formalistic deviations.

Evidently connected to Terentiev's theatrical activity is the play *Iordano Bruno,* attached to the last letter sent from Leningrad to Zdanevich. The play is the only theatrical work-outline of Terentiev that has made it to us, although it is presumable that other plays were present in that "*pood*" of poems and various manuscripts, never traced, which we read about in the letter.

A Note on a Letter

This theatre of the absurd presents all the typical procedures of Terentiev's "alogical" writing. In the jokes made by characters, phrases in pure zaum alternate with entire propositions of complete meaning, some of which seem to have a slight logical connection between them, which creates the illusion of a rationality of the absurd and invites the spectator, with clear derisive intent, to a "common" effort to understand the text. The same procedure can be seen within the zaum sentences, where, among pure sound sequences, resting on a consonant or a dominant vowel, single Russian or foreign words are set, with a similar sound, often in phonetic rendering, or a series of Russian synophones which are formed into examples of "internal declension" *à la* Khlebnikov (for example, the sequences "*rad ryad rod / dyra dar dur*"). Further ambiguities, and therefore pluralities of sense in nonsense, are obtained through the deformation of the pronunciation of words, Russian or foreign (for example in a joke by Schmetterlink the words "*shetch, shetch*!," which, with allusion to the story and together with the situation outlined, can be deformations both of "*zhech,*" to burn, and of "*sech,*" to cut, to tear apart), or through nonsensical associations of words that slip one into the other, creating internal phenomena of *sdvig* [shift] (for example, in "polisadsudpali").

An effect of contamination, of space and time, and of different areas of human creativity,[10] is obtained both with the name of the place where

the tragedy takes place (the Place de la Concorde
that, with a reference to the guillotine, transfers the
action to the epoch of the French Revolution) and
with the names of the characters (Schmetterlink,
which brings to mind both Maurice Maeterlinck
and Klemens von Metternich. As well as other
historically specific images; Giordano Bruno, Mona
Lisa Gioconda and Kolumbia). A representation of the
spirit of the 41° and of Terentiev's "nihilism" is made
clear in the final scene: absurd, bloody and boring,
but also vaguely erotic.

 A Note on a Letter

1 An edited and partial translation of Giovanna Pagani Cesa, 'Une Lettera di Igor Terent'ev a Il'ja Zdanevič', *L'Avanguardia a Tiflis*, Quaderni del Seminario di Iranistica, Uralo-Altaistica e Caucasologia dell' Università degli Studi di Venezia, edited by L. Magarotto, M. Marzaduri, and G. P. Cesa, Venice, 1982, pp. 269-280.

2 These letters, alongside the other surviving letters of Terentiev are published in *Igor Terentiev, Sobraniye Sochineniye* [Collected Works], edited by Marzio Marzaduri and Tatyana Nikolskaya, S. Eurasiatica: Quaderni del Dipartimento di Studi Eurasiatici Universita degli Studi Venezia, Bologna, 1988, pp. 395-414.

3 Referring to Boris Arvatov, 'Language Creation' [Rechetvorchestvo], *Russian Futurisms through Its Manifestos, 1912-1928*, edited and translated by Anna Lawton and Herbert Eagle, Cornell University Press, 1988, pp. 217-231. Arvatov's text originally published in *Lef No. 2*, 1923.

4 From Terentiev's letter to Zdanevich sent from Moscow on May 4th 1923, published for the first time in Igor Terentiev, *Sobranie Sochinenii*, Bologna, 1988, pp. 398-399. Here Terentiev refers to their manifesto stating that "Company 41° unifies left-wing Futurism, and affirms *zaum* as the mandatory form for the embodiment of art." 'Manifesto of 41°', in *Russian Futurism Through Its Manifestos*, p. 177.

5 Apart from Kruchenkykh and Terentiev, the second, April-May, issue of *Lef* journal published in 1923 included poems on May Day by Vladimir Mayakovsky, Boris Pasternak, Vasily Kamensky and others. In the same issue of the *Lef* journal, Terentiev also published a short text on leftist Futurism in Caucasia, reporting on activities of the group 41° and Zdanevich's activities in Paris. Igor Terentiev, 'Lef Zakavkazya (Kompaniya 41°) ['Lef in Transcaucasia (The Company of the 41°)'], *Lef, No. 2*, 1923, p. 177.

6 Published in the third issue of *Lef*, Terentiev's open letter was a rejoinder to Sosnovksy's slander of the Futurists from the Caucasia published in *Pravda* on April 23rd 1923. "Sosnovsky informs the readers that we, Zdanevich, Kruchenykh and Terentiev, 'rushed away from the Red Army.'
This is not true: 1) Zdanevich left Tbilisi for Paris under the Mensheviks, and a year and a half before their disappearance. 2) Kruchenykh 'rushed' not away from Tbilisi, but to meet the Red Army (in Baku). 3) Terentiev travelled to Constantinople with a Soviet passport, and before his

A Note on a Letter

departure and after his return from abroad, he worked in the Red Army as an artist and writer.

I believe that the facts that are well known locally (Baku-Tbilisi) should be approached more seriously by an employee of the central press and not be carried away to the point of slander by the slogan – 'beat the Futurists'." Igor Terentiev, 'Otkroy pis'mo' [Open Letter], *Lef, No. 3*, 1923, p. 5.

7 Alexei Kruchenykh soon gave up the name *41°* to speak of a "transrational school" [zaumnaja shkola], in which he included many other protagonists of the Russian avant-garde. In his writings, the name *41°* appears for the last time in the book *Fonetika Teatra,* published in 1924.

8 Aleksandr Tufanov (1877–1943) was a poet and philologist known for his research on the 'phonetics of poetry'. He was founder of Orden Zaumnikov [Order of Zaumniks], one of the initiators of *Oberiu,* and the author of *K Zaumi: Fonicheskaya muzika b funkzii soglasnikh fonem* [Towards Zaum: Phonic Music as a Function of Consonant Phonemes, 1924]. Geoffrey F. Cebula, 'Alexander Tufanov's "Ushkuiniki", Historicist "Zaum", and the Creation of Oberiu', *The Slavic and Eastern European Journal, Vol. 51, No. 1,* Spring 2014, pp. 93-112. Sergei Sigov, 'Red Zaumnika' [Order of Zaumniks],

Pojmovnik Ruske Avangarde Vol. 5, Zagreb, 1985, pp. 117-130.

9 In this regard there is the testimony, however ambiguous, of Konstantin Paustovsky who in his memoirs names, among the people he frequented in Tbilisi "… the painter Terentiev, who had made the first attempt to bring the theatre to the city squares…" K. Paustovsky, *Brosok na jug,* in *Sobraniye Sochineniy,* Moscow, 1968, p. 382.

10 "One of the devices Terentiev used in his writings was based on contamination, often aligned to lapsus, where meaning is usually constructed through the context." Tatyana Nikolskaya, 'Igor Terentjev/Zaum', *Pojmovnik Ruske Avangarde, Vol. 3*, 1985, p. 212.

A Note on a Letter

Igor Terentiev's
Letter to Ilya Zdanevich

Including
the Tragedy
Iordano Bruno

February 5th 1924, Leningrad

Dear Ilya! I sent you at least four letters from the USSR, but have only received one of yours in 2 1/2 years.[1] I have been petitioning for your prestige in Russia and pouring no water onto Lef's mill, except for the poem 'May Tay Day' [Melt May Lay],[2] which contains not a drop of water! Kruchenykh has in fact been mesmerised by Lef and is unwilling to support 41°. He thinks Lef itself is flowing onto our mill! He is right to some extent, because Lef cannot part ways with zaum and must support it out of a sense of self-preservation – as the halo of Futurism amid new-fangled theorists, it drove sycophants and freeloaders from all their holes and burrows. I left Moscow five months ago exactly because working with Lefovites, despite their magnificent attitude to my person, is utter nonsense of the order of legalising haemorrhoids.[3] Here in Leningrad, at the former Myatlev House (2 Pomchatskaya Street), I have two rooms allocated to 41°: a study adorned, furnished and clad in 41 degrees, and a sound workshop![4] For several months, up to ten young people have been working with me – musicians, actors and engineers (to be). In a few days, with the title "Phonological Unit of the Research Institute for Higher Artistic Knowledge," this work is being presented at the Academic Centre.[5] Materials for the publication of "Bulletin of the Research I.H.A.K." have been prepared.[6] Please write, in the

   Igor Terentiev's Letter to Ilya Zdanevich

most detailed possible terms, of your work in Paris and send it along with all materials and printing instructions. Parts of the Institute (90%) are united by the platform of 'Non-objectivity' and comprise a federation: 41[0] + Suprematism (Malevich) + Zorved[7] (Matyushin).[8] In Leningrad, I read up to 14-17 lectures, in each of which I mentioned you and read your poetry. Kruchenykh has published 5-6 brochures![9] This is no small effort, and in this regard he does not deserve any title of "lazy beast." Publishing overall is very hard (pricey), for me in particular: you know that in Tbilisi – *I was not* the publisher! As of now – the amount of poetry and miscellaneous manuscripts has run up to about a pood.[10] Consequently, soon, one way or another – I shall get myself published. Here is the material: if you could publish my book called *OPTAC*.[11] An introductory article + several poems + the *Iordano Bruno* tragedy. Please write the article yourself using typographic techniques, the main points being thus:

1. 41° — new encyclopaedism (Rousseau—Voltaire—Diderot et cetera) except that our encyclopaedia is perpendicular, not horizontal

M   mneniye [sentiment] etc.
         mnemosine – mother of muses etc.
         mnemonics – science of memory etc.
         mnimiye [imaginary] numbers etc.

    Igor Terentiev's Letter to Ilya Zdanevich

our direction ↓
old direction →

One who is unable to understand language in the perpendicular direction is illiterate!

2. Optimism = optovaya torgovlya [wholesale] = optical instruments

$1^2 + 2 = 3$ $= 11°$ = inorganic world
$2^2 + 1 = 5$ $= 21°$ = animal kingdom
$3^2 + 1 = 10$ $= 31°$ = individualism
$4^2 + 1 = 17$ $= 41°$ = wholesale.

3. We have power over "proper names": Plyushkin, Tolstoyevsky, Durgeniy [*Fool Genius/Turgenev*]. "Proper names" are theft! Nationalisation of language + internationalisation = optimism!

4. Statistics + crystallography = 41° method for words.

5. Exact knowledge = knowledge of the point.
World = system of reflections.
Le ferme Esprit = sense of touch = reality guarantee № 1.
sight = № 2.
hearing = № 3.
zaum = № 4.

quadruple reflection = 41°
triple » = 31°
double » = 21°
single » = 11°

55   Igor Terentiev's Letter to Ilya Zdanevich

The sensed object = le ferme Esprit = warmth has its tangible mirrors, its space.

6. Contemporary culture is a hodgepodge of Chopin – Schopenhauer – Einstein – Steiner etc.

7. The individual world of objects has reached its end! Competition with wholesale culture is – for hobbyists, petty sellers and other particularists – impossible!

8. We (41°) have our own territory (sonic space) and our own time (tangible) in the perpendicular!

Here's the tragedy, *Iordano Bruno*.

> A crowded space. A lonely time. A simple act. Schmetterlink and wife Kolumbia are crossing the Place de la Concorde. Iordano is sitting in the centre with his work. Curious, the couple stop.

Iordano: rad ryad rod (reading in a presentational tone) dyra dar dur.[12]
Kolumbia: I shall report to the pope because this is happening near our house.
Schmetterlink: Go to hell (Kolumbia exits).
Iordano: You Moochenigo[13] Niol Aluy Likinspikindicopernicus. S*i*hu! Sakhan! Z*a*kan! Soup!
Schmetterlink: I shall go and call up a few more people! (Takes a bow, leaves and comes back).
Schmetterlink: I have brought all of humanity!

   Igor Terentiev's Letter to Ilya Zdanevich

Humanity (entering): Gun ATA NOUGAT
          EHEH UFULUMPPPFFSS!
          KiriPIKIT BLUNT FLUFF
          HOP PARAIK KAKA!
          Ukuku! Zaf trik trak!

Iordano: Bridano lyes plis!
kindle grab![14]
drawinge figur!

Humanity: Guru gund ubunt agugom polisadcourt
pourt small slam.
Hihipihihi thunder ignoramba gromba duromba
turgrahahaah!
Ndunda![15]

Police (entering on all fours):
          PUNDA PAPAPA PAL
          DONDA DODODO
          TO TO
          BAPT
          BOUGHT
          ILL
          GEN
          IES
          DOZE
          EAR
          PINTOR[16]

Kolumbia: Boom
          baga
          ior
          dana
          shmoke sizzl scratching zippo ippope![17]

Schmetterlink: Shmoke, shmoke![18]

   Igor Terentiev's Letter to Ilya Zdanevich

Iordano: Moochenigo!
Humanity, Iordano, Schmetterlink, Kolumbia:
Scratchitch! Guilloteen! Hal ya ha lya ho KOM!
(They erect a gallows. Schmetterlink grabs a sword.
Iordano lowers head and says a word.)
Iordano: I love everybody and everybody loves me.
        I die like Osiristus and the Archichrist!
        I love everybody and everybody rowres me.
(everyone but Iordano and Schmetterlink exits
suddenly and decisively.)
Iordano: She Shefot shevayola?[19]
Schmetterlink: Stomach … ? Don't follow.
Iordano: RUFFLE! SHUFFLE!
Schmetterlink: Shudder?
Iordano: SHTUPID!
Schmetterlink: They left! Did they really think I cut
your head off. Anyway, given humanity's negligent
attitude to capital punishment – I shall not be cutting
your head.
Girl (running onstage): Lady sent 100 rubles.
        Buy what you like.
        Do not buy white or black.
        No don't say it.
        What do you want to buy!?
Iordano: O Mararakuli!
Schmetterlink (to girl): Shooshoosh![20] Know this: we
have nothing else!
Iordano: Thia! Divinsa![21]
Schmetterlink: The mood is so feeble, this will be a
way out of the situation.
Come here my girl! (looking to stab her).

    Igor Terentiev's Letter to Ilya Zdanevich

Girl: I'm telling mum what you've been talking about.
Schmetterlink: Quiet!
Kolumbia (running onstage): No, don't be quiet, the bastards deserve this!
Girl: AAH ILIOTIA UIOUOAEI
Lady (Monna Lisa Gioconda): What is wrong my girl?
Girl: U O A E I E A O U Y I I I!

SEMOC YTINAMUH
(returns to the shout of "humanity comes")

Humanity: What Happened?
(10 minutes of deathly silence
grows the letter Y!)
Schmetterlink: Iordano Bruno murdered his own daughter.
Monks (appearing):
    Entertechnica Crucitarnibus
    Expiranda[22] Castolimus
    CABBAGE
    NOSE

(Iordano Bruno burned at the stake)
Choir sings:

GUNUS TSVI TOMINE
DERE MORAMOR[23] ILLE
KUYUS CROAKIMUS[24]
anima
gerdano
finita la tragedia.

1 Before this letter, Terentiev sent four letters to Ilya Zdanevich from the Soviet Union, which he recalls. Some days later, on February 16th, Kruchenykh sent a letter to Zdanevich, thanking him for *lidantIU fAram* [1923].

2 Refers to Igor Terentiev, '1-oe maya' [May 1st], *Lef No. 3*, 1923, p. 17.

"Melt,
May!
Lay
a drop
to drink
– let
love –
to the rocks.
The working class.
Dry
they lived.
This son
of a father
has no place.
Be
May,
with me.
May
be
upon you.
Lay
your hand
in mine.
Let's
smoke.
I, brother,
say
to convey
labour.
Poet
Therefore
pensive
PIGASUS.
And you
from the tops
of the chimneys
lay
some change
for May.
My felicitations."

3 In *Traktat o Sploshnom Neprilichi* [Treatise on Total Obscenity, 1920], Terentiev writes about "hemorrhoidal heights of the theory of knowledge," a quote taken from Vladimir Markov, *Russian Futurism: A History*, University of California Press, 1968, p. 360.

4 In the Myatlev House on Saint Isaac's Square in Leningrad the Museum of Artistic Culture was founded and later transformed into the State Institute of Artistic Culture (GINKhUK), where Terentiev opened his Phonological Department and Laboratory.

5 The opening of the phonological laboratory was announced to the press at the end of November 1923: "The Research Institute will open two more departments in the near future: on the technique of painting, which will be in the charge of Pavel Mansurov, teacher at the Academy of Arts, and on phonetics, with classes conducted by linguist Igor Terentiev," *Zhizn' iskusstva* [Life of Art], No. 47,

 Igor Terentiev's Letter to Ilya Zdanevich

1923, p. 25. Very little is known about the activities of this department; documents have disappeared, and available evidence and memoirs are rare and contradictory. Collaborating with Terentiev at the Phonological Institute were Alexander Vvedensky, future founder of the OBERIU group, Alexander Tufanov, a zaum theoretician, and composer M. Druskin. The only available sources are *Iz materialov Fonologicheskogo otdela GINKhUKa. Vstupitel'naya stat'i i publikatsiya Galiny Demosfenovoy* [From the materials of the Phonological Department of GINKhUK. An introductory article and publication by Galina Demosfenova], *Terent'yevskiy sbornik*, edited by Sergey Kudriavtsev, Hylea, Moscow, 1996, pp. 110-126; Terentiev's letter to Kruchenykh sent from Leningrad on December 23rd 1923, in Igor Terentiev, *Sobraniye Sochineniy* [Collected Works], edited by Marzio Marzaduri and Tatyana Nikolskaya, S. Eurasiatica: Quaderni del Dipartimento di Studi Eurasiatici Universita degli Studi Venezia, Bologna, 1988, pp. 400-404; Vera S. Pilgun, 'Fonologicheskiy otdel Instituta khudozhestvennoy kul'tury pod rukovodstvom I.G. Terent'yeva' [The Phonological Department of the Institute of Artistic Culture under the direction of I.G. Terentiev]', *Observatoriya Kul'tury 19: 4*, 2022, pp. 410-417.

6 The Bulletin of the Research Institute of Higher Artistic Knowledge was never published. The Institute of Higher Artistic Knowledge was one of the names Malevich proposed for the State Institute of Artistic Culture; the other potential name was the Research Institute of Artistic Labour. Pamela Kachurin, 'Malevich as Soviet Bureaucrat: Ginkhuk and the Survival of the Avant-Garde, 1924-1926', *Rethinking Malevich*, edited by C. Douglas & C. Lodder, The Pindar Press, London, 2007, p. 126.
Malevich was the director of GINKhUK, whose prescience in adapting Suprematism to the curriculum of the new research objectives, contributed to the survival of the Institute.

7 Zorved, or zorkoye vedeniye [seeing knowledge], was the group headed by Mikhail Matyushin, a long-time collaborator of Malevich.

8 The ideas of Terentiev during the GINKhUK period echoed the experiments of Kruchenykh, Malevich, and Matyushin in 1913, who, together with Velimir Khlebnikov staged the zaum opera *Victory Over the Sun*. Terentiev described his project as grounding these previous abstract experiments into the "materialist" understanding. Igor Terentiev, 'Tezisy' [Theses, 1923-24], *Sobraniye Sochineniy*, 1988, p. 433.

   Igor Terentiev's Letter to Ilya Zdanevich

9 Kruchenykh published mainly theoretical works in 1923, in which certain ideas of the 41° were again put forward: three books published under the imprint of the MAF [Moscow Association of Futurists]: *Faktura slova* [Texture of the Word], *Svidologiya Russkogo Stiha* [Shiftology of Russian Verse] and *Apokalipsis v Russkoi Literature* [Apocalypse in Russian Literature]; as 41° editions: *Sobstvennyye rasskazy, stikhi i pesni dlya detey* [Original stories, poems and songs for children] and *Fonetika teatra* [Phonetics of the Theatre].

10 An archaic measure of weight equal to 16.38kg.

11 ОПТАК [OPTAK] was never published. Terentiev worked feverishly in those years, as the hints scattered throughout his letters attest, but all this material has in all likelihood been lost. Of particular interest here is the "tragedy" *Iordano Bruno*. Indeed, while theoretical observations renew the 41° theses about "perpendicular language" – in this play Terentiev arranged events in free space and time in the spirit of Malevich (from whose theories Terentiev also derives the idea of zaum as the "fourth dimension").

12 "Rad ryad rod" could be adapted as a "joyous row gender [race]," "dyra dar dur" as "hole, the gift of fools." [Translator's note.]

"Dyra" could be read as a reference to Kruchenykh's pivotal zaum poem from 1913 'Dyr bul shchyl', which Terentiev described in 1924 as a "hole to the future" [dyra v budushcheye], Igor Terentiev, 'Kto Lef, Kto Praf' [Whose Left, Whose Right, 1924], *Sobraniye Sochineniy*, p. 288.

13 In the original, it says 'Mochenigo', which is a combination of 'muchenik' [martyr] and Giovanni Mocenigo, the patrician who invited Giordano Bruno to Venice in 1591, and who later denounced him to the Inquisition.

14 In the original, "rugami vest znop" could be adapted as "rukami vzyat' snop" = take[s] a clump of hay. [Translator's note.]
Boris Konstriktor in his 'deconstructivist' reading of *Iordano Bruno*, suggested that "rugami" alludes to insult, and that he related to the rejection of "official in legal and moral aspects." Boris Konstriktor, 'Tragediya Igorya Ternet'yeva *Jordano Bruno*: opyt strukturnogo preskaza' [The Tragedy of Igor Terentiev *Iordano Bruno*: experiment of structural retelling], *Terentievsky Sbornik*, edited by Sergey Kudriavtsev, Hylea, Moscow, 1996, p. 69.

15 Konstriktor reads this as "the crowd pronouncing the verdict: 'Ndunda!'," in Russian close to "erunda" meaning "nonsense."

   Igor Terentiev's Letter to Ilya Zdanevich

Konstriktor, 'Tragediya Igorya Ternet'yeva *Jordano Bruno*', p. 70. Another possible rendering of "ndunda" is "do dna," meaning "to the bottom."

16 Multiple possible interpretations of puntik= putnik [traveller] + punktik [point]. [Translator's note.]

17 The original says "shetch shivo," which could be adapted as "szhech' yego zhivo" = burn him alive. [Translator's note.]

18 As in the previous line, "shetch" can allude to "zhech," to burn, and to "sech," to cut, to tear apart; "sech" also can mean whipping as a form of corporal punishment, hence the sonically similar to "scratch." Scratch also fits well with the following sarcastic proposal "Pocheshika" = scratch that itch!
     Konstriktor interpreted these phonetic screeches as, "Hissing sounds emphasise that the characters are not speaking with their own voices. The Imperial Security Machine starts broadcasting." Konstriktor, 'Tragediya Igorya Ternet'yeva *Jordano Bruno*', p. 72.

19 "Zhivot zhivoye" = belly alive. [Translator's note.]

20 "Ididitida" could be a deformation of "idi otsyuda" = go away. [Translator's note.]

21 Thea, Divina both mean "divine" [feminine] in Old Greek and Latin.

22 "Omiranda" = umirat' = to die. [Translator's note.]

23 Mors [death], amor [love] in Latin. [Translator's note.]

24 "Akalitimus" = okolet' = to die. [Translator's note.]

     Igor Terentiev's Letter to Ilya Zdanevich

The
Orchestral Lives

Ketevan S. Kintsurashvili

In one of his memoirs, Ilya Zdanevich mentions
that Tiflis [Tbilisi], the city of his birth, located
at 44.82° longitude and 41.71° latitude, stretches
along the banks of the river Mtkvari, and that it was
once the capital of the Kingdom of Kartli, whose
origins predate Christianity. In the 18th century,
the Georgians, exhausted by endless battles
with neighbouring Persia and Turkey, sought the
protection of the Russian kings, but at the very first
favourable opportunity, the latter turned Georgia into
one of their provinces. Tiflis became the residence
of the Russian viceroy — i.e. of whichever general
or prince would rule, unchecked, over this remote
province of the Russian Empire. Schools, institutions:
everything was rapidly Russianized, including
the local inhabitants. On the other hand, these
conditions raised Tiflis to a much higher level than
any other provincial Russian city in terms of cultural
development. Tiflis became a unique mixture of
metropolitan capital and remote province.[1]

***

The atmosphere in Georgia during the second half
of the 1910s was very favourable for an avant-garde
movement. Busy with a chain of difficult historical
events – the wars and revolutions – Russia was
constantly distracted, and unable to focus on its
outlying provinces, and from 1916 onwards many
artists, writers and poets began to head south, where
they were welcomed with open arms by the local

      The Orchestral Lives

artistic and literary circles. At the time, Georgia was enjoying its short-lived independence (1918-1921), and the country offered a perfect environment for the development of art and literature. Indeed, artistic life was at its peak in Georgia in those days.

The epithet of 'fantastic' can often be heard regarding the avant-garde in Tiflis. It is linked to the name of the first café in Tiflis – ფანტასტიკური დუქანი [Fantastikuri Dukhani, Fantastic Inn], opened in 1917 on the initiative of poet Yury Degen. The café could accommodate ten to fifty people. Alexei Kruchenykh used to call this place the 'Parnassus of Tiflis', and it was sometimes compared to the Cabaret Voltaire in Zürich.

The Fantastic Inn had its own muse – Sofia Melnikova, an actress at Tiflis' Miniature Theatre, who recited poems and danced at the café. Melnikova's own salon in Tiflis, the სპილენძის ქვაბი [Spilendzis qvabi, Copper Pot], was the pot in which many avant-garde ideas simmered and were prepared. Ilya Zdanevich was not indifferent towards her, and it was to her that he dedicated his second 'dra', асЁл напракАт [Asiol na Prokat, Donkey for Rent]. Ilya decided to publish this 'dra' himself and to present Melnikova with a copy, and later various representatives of the Tiflis avant-garde also contributed with works to an album dedicated to her at his initiative. The result was the creation of probably the most avant-garde album of its kind from the Tiflis scene.

Melnikova's album contains works produced by many different artists during the years 1917 and

The Orchestral Lives

1919. The book opens with a portrait of Melnikova
by Polish artist Zygmunt Waliszewski, followed
by poems written by Nina Vasilyeva and Tatiana
Vechorka. It also features a paper on the Persian
influence on Georgian manuscripts between the 16th
and 18th centuries by Dmitri Gordeev. Gordeev's
work is followed by Ilya's асЁл напракАт (with three
illustrations by him, including two larger ones which
were glued and folded into the book); Futurist
poems in Armenian by Kara Darvish, an Armenian
artist from Tiflis; Убийство на романтической почве
[Ubiistvo na romanticheskoi pochve, Murder for
Romantic Reasons] by Vasily Katanian; a poem by
Alexei Kruchenykh; poems in Georgian by Grigol
Robakidze, Tsitsian Tabidze and Paolo Iashvili; a
toast to Melnikova by Igor Terentiev; and poems by
Alexandr Chachikov, Nikolai Cherniavsky and Grigory
Shaikevich. Also glued into Melnikova's album were
works by Aleksandr Bazhbeuk-Melikyan, Zygmunt
Waliszewski, Kirill Zdanevich, Natalia Goncharova,
Lado Gudiashvili, Mikhail Kalashnikov and Igor
Terentiev, as well as printed graphic works by Ilya.
The album also includes a list of public talks given
by Futurists in the Fantastic Inn, the Imedi café and
the Tiflis Conservatoire, as well as a bibliography of
the books and articles they published between 1917
and 1919. Ilya thus brought together all the works that
were produced around Melnikova and the Fantastic
Inn over the years. Kirill Zdanevich contributed a
painting of a crown in Indian ink for the book's cover,
and six small drawings as illustrations for different

The Orchestral Lives

poems. Ilya was responsible for the design of the book, whose typefaces and fonts immediately attract the reader's attention. Ilya self-financed and published 180 copies of Melnikova's album.

Initially, the Fantastic Inn was called პოეტთა სტუდია [Poetta studia, The Poet's Studio] or პოეტების ახალი ცეხი [Poetebis akhali tsekhi, A New Workshop of Poets], in response to the Workshop of Poets in St. Petersburg – and was home to Neo-Acmeists. The poet Sergey Gorodetsky and his local Guild of Poets played a leading role here. This group made friends with the union ცისფერი ყანწები [Tsisperi Kantsebi, Blue Horns] and notably with its leading poet-members such as Valerian Gaprindashvili, Paolo Iashvili and Titsian Tabidze, known as სამი ქართველი ძმა [Sami qartveli dzma, The Three Georgian brothers]. Parallel to this, the so-called 'Three Idiots': Ilya Zdanevich, Alexei Kruchenykh, and Igor Terentiev, founded a ფუტურისტთა სინდიკატი [Futuristta sindikati, Futurist Syndicate] and ფუტურიზმის უნივერსიტეტი [Futurismis universiteti, Futurist University] here. Under the name of the Futurist University, numerous conferences dedicated to Futurism and zaum poetry were held at the Fantastic Inn. Other cafés in Tiflis were as follows: ფარშევანგის კუდი [Parshevangis Kudi, The Peacock's Tail], ძმური ნუგეში [Dzmuri Nugeshi, The Brotherly Consolation], ჭიქა ჩაი [Tchika Chai, A Cup of Tea], არგონავტის ნავი [Argonavtis Navi, The Argonauts' Sail], იმედი [Imedi,

Hope], ინტერნაციონალი [Internatsionali, The International], ქართული კლუბი [Qartuli Klubi, The Georgian Club], ქიმერიონი [Kimerioni, Chimera] and so on. A new tradition of interior painting was present from the very beginning.

In November 1917, Ilya Zdanevich, Kruchenykh and Terentiev founded a new association and named it 41° (an allusion to the longitude of Tiflis and the highest degree of alcohol and of the human body's temperature).

In 1913 the Zdanevich brothers, together with their friends, the artists Mikhaïl Le Dentu and Mikhail Larionov, created Everythingism. They announced in their manifesto that they supported all movements in art and literature, past or present. When Kirill Zdanevich's personal exhibition was held in Tiflis in 1917, Ilya Zdanevich and Alexei Kruchenykh described his paintings as Оркестровая живопись [Orchestral paintings], similar to Ilya's *Orchestral poetry*, which again implied a musical merger of numerous sources.

Sergei Sudeikin, the famous Russian scenographer, who came from St. Petersburg to Georgia together with his wife Vera Sudeikina in 1919, was invited by the group of Georgian poets to paint the walls of a café ქიმერიონი [Kimerioni, Chimera]. Sudeikin took up the artistic theme of theatre and theatricality, the masquerade and masks, clowns, dancers, monsters, chimaeras, characters of Commedia dell'Arte, etc. Artistically transformed portraits of the "cast of characters" of the café were depicted on the walls too. David Kakabadze and Lado

Gudiashvili also created additional wall paintings in the interior of the café.

In 1919, the influential spiritual teacher George Gurdjieff and his wife arrived in Tiflis. His disciples and followers assembled around him. They were composer Thomas de Hartmann and his wife Olga Schumacher, stage designer Alexander von Salzmann and his wife Jeanne Matignon. Matignon taught Georgian youth how to dance based on the method of Émile Jaques-Dalcroze. She later ceded her studio to Gurdjieff, who opened The Institute for the Harmonious Development of Man in the studio and she became his assistant. Salzmann painted decorations, Hartmann played the piano, and Olga made costumes. Kirill Zdanevich and Igor Terentiev also used to attend Gurdjieff's lessons. In 1919, Terentiev wrote in the only newspaper published by the 41° association: "The Gurdjieff method is twice as rich as that of Dalcroze."[2]

In 1920 Ilya was granted permission to study in Paris, and after publishing his fourth 'dra', Зга якабы [zgA YAkaby, As if Zga], he sailed (in steerage class) to Istanbul. Here he prepared his fifth 'dra' for publication. Towards the end of 1921 Kirill and Ilya met again in Istanbul. Kirill was on his way home from Paris, and Ilya was on his way there. In February 1921, shortly after Kirill's return, the Bolshevik flag flew over Tiflis. Georgia's independence had been snatched away, and the country's Menshevik government was on its way to exile in France. By the end of October Ilya was granted his visa and

     The Orchestral Lives

in November of 1921 he had arrived in Paris. In the
winter of 1922, Kirill returned to Istanbul with Igor
Terentiev. They tried to obtain either an American or
a French visa in order to take their 41° project abroad
and to continue working on it with Ilya, but this never
transpired.

The Orchestral Lives

1 Ilya Zdanevich, *Notes,* 1927, p.
6. The notebook with a yellowed
cardboard cover, red spine,
checked pages and the margins
drawn by a red pencil. Kept in
Iliazd's archive, the property of
François Mairé.

2 Igor Ternetiev, 'Vecher Zhanni
Matinioni i Gurjieva' [The
Evening of Jeanne Matignon
and Gurdjieff], *41°,* 1919, 14–20
July, p.4.

TERENTIEV

,
a man
who
walked
vertically

Adam Ranđelović

Igor Terentiev, that bald man with the "athletic voice"
(that's how he himself called his baritone), an excellent
dancer, a good actor, the "most radically left of all the
left-wing" theatre directors of the young Soviet Union,
a brilliant poet and playwright, one of the founders
(together with Kirill Zdanevich, Ilya Zdanevich and
Alexei Kruchenykh) of the avant-garde group 41° in
Tbilisi (then Tiflis), deconstructivist and formalist, self-
proclaimed President of Fluids, failed craftsman, failed
proletarian, "a man who walked vertically," was shot in
April 1937 in Butyrka prison in Moscow — seven years
before the date he set for himself back in Georgia,
in his second collection of poetry, *Fact*, where he
predicted his death would come in 1944, as follows:

Igor Terentiev
1892–1944

As was the case for many others (Osip Mandelstam,
for example), it was believed for a long time that he
died of a heart disease "somewhere in the labour
camps" in 1941. That's what his daughter was told
after her father's official rehabilitation during de-
Stalinization in the second half of the 1980s.

In the 1970s it was believed that Terentiev
was still alive, but in hiding, using someone else's
name — it's no wonder that something mythical still
surrounds his name.

Terentiev's poetic heritage — which, in addition
to the ideas of Boris Eikhenbaum, Yury Tynyanov
and Viktor Shklovsky (from the Russian formalist

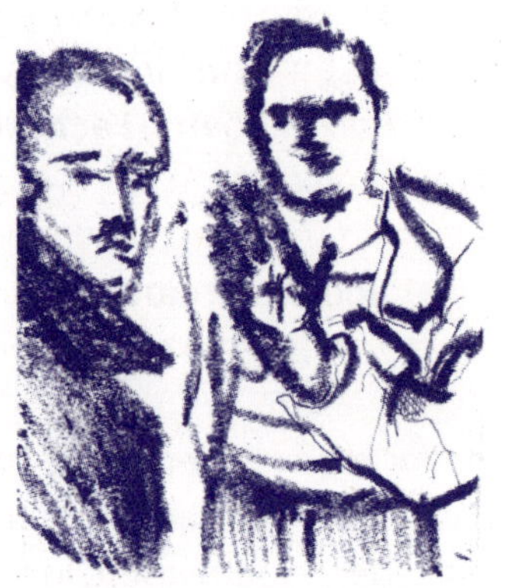

With nobody's appreciation — of his own kind nature alone —
Ilya became a poet.

 Terentiev, a man who walked vertically

school, OPOJAZ), that formed his radical and unique theatrical style — is not to be neglected.

Let's go back in time a little.

In 1918, after two years attempting unsuccessfully to find a job, he joined the avant-garde group 41° in Tbilisi (a city that became home for many Russian intellectuals after the beginning of Russian Civil War). There, in just three years he would publish several books of poems, manifestos and theory on zaum (which he honed as a radical poetic practice of chance and accident in art, as a deliberate anti-stylism, a "plagiarism," Luddism, citationism, rhythm and unravelling of the phonetic battle of words, similar to phenomenological reduction).

At the same time, Terentiev was fully aware that zaum was not and never would be a language outright: "Zaum is a decisive condition for the creation of a linguistic international!"

LIVAL RPATA
PTK PTK PTK

He himself would call the group "superfuturistic," and Georges Ribemont-Dessaignes (the French Dadaist and Surrealist) would characterise them as a "Russian type of literary Dadaism."

At the beginning of the twenties he left Tbilisi, in an unsuccessful attempt to escape to France. In the summer of 1923 he moved to Petrograd, where he worked in a museum, together with Kazimir Malevich, Mikhail Matyushin and Pavel Filonov.

Excited by the works of Vsevolod Meyerhold and Vladimir Mayakovsky, Terentiev made his first professional theatrical outings at the Agitstudio of the Red Theater ("the first Soviet working-class theatre," as Terentiev was calling it, was founded by Viktor Shimanovsky in 1918), where he directed his own play *John Reed*. In Georgia, Terentiev was involved in amateur puppet shows, developing a theatrical sense of criticism towards Western European logocentrism, similar to that of Antonin Artaud. Even back then he was aware that Futurism was struggling to find adequate scenic tools, and was merely expanding the theatrical palette of the symbolists.

John Reed was written the same year (1924), as his most famous, and probably best play (or, as Ilya Zdanevich would call it — "dra") *Iordano Bruno*, a piece of zaum paroxysms.

He then founded the experimental *Teatr Doma Pechati* [Theatre of the House of Press] in the Shuvalov Palace on the Fontanka Embankment. There, in the short period of two years that the theatre would exist, he created his directorial masterpiece based on Gogol's 'The Government Inspector' (it premiered in 1927 and had three versions). He "collided two discourses" as part of his "sound-movement" method ("Building a theatre on a sound, slightly supplementing it with visual material," as he would describe, because the words were "moved" into sounds, thus giving a wider frame of reference to each "line"): Gogol's intact text (Terentiev intentionally did not intervene) was deconstructed with the added phonetic commentary, which apostrophized the sheer formality of a plot.

For Terentiev (and for Russian Formalists), sound had to be viewed as a "physical phenomenon," a more aggressive way to forcibly stimulate perception, thus it is more effective for the delivery of information, and "ceasing the automatic process of 'comprehension'."

Scenic representation for him was synonymous to deconstruction, and he had already done something similar, back in Georgia, but with his typographical experiments with words.

For example, Terentiev's Khlestakov (a character in 'The Government Inspector') spoke his most famous monologue – Munchausenesque stream of consciousness – while sinking into sleep. Why? "Khlestakov has been telling the lie of that monologue, on the stage boards, for so many years that he is tired of it."

His staging of Gogol's play was, of course, a very strong statement, a playful, but merciless answer to Meyerhold — his former "teacher." While Terentiev opened a new chapter in theatrical experimentation, Meyerhold's 'The Government Inspector' was an end of his era for his "left techniques."

Nevertheless, in 1928, during Teatr Doma Pechati's visit to the Meyerhold Theatre, Anatoly Lunacharsky offered to move Terentiev's troupe to Moscow. They failed to find a venue and the money, so the ensemble broke up. At around the same time, the director of Dom Pechati was arrested in Daniil Kharms' apartment.

⅘   Terentiev, a man who walked vertically

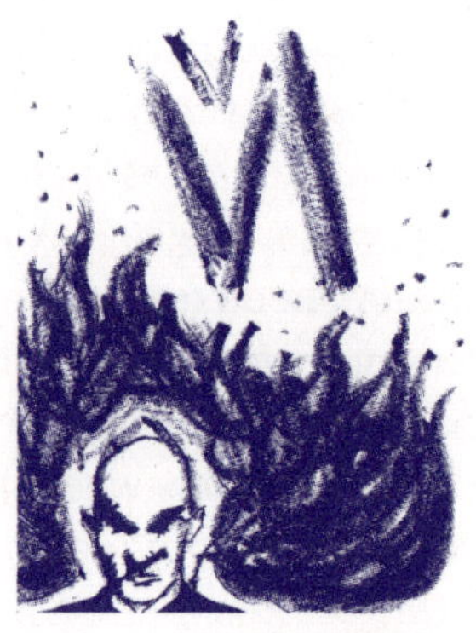

10 minutes of deathly silence grows the letter Y!

 Terentiev, a man who walked vertically

Terentiev founded the Anti-Khudozhestvenny Teatr (the Anti-Artistic Theatre, as opposed to Konstantin Stanislavsky's Moscow Art Theatre, famous for its naturalism), staging *War and Peace* in the context of Lenin's text about the "historical sin of Tolstoyism." Soon, the theatre collapsed, and Terentiev moved to Ukraine, where he was originally from. He worked in Odessa, then he established the Ukrainian Youth Theatre in Dnipropetrovsk, and was arrested in 1931. Terentiev, who couldn't stand any form of violence, immediately confessed to everything that he was accused of. The death penalty was replaced by five years in a forced labour camp at the very last moment. Allegedly, before being taken to be shot, he explained to investigators how one could obtain the desired information during interrogation, without using physical violence.

His statements during the interrogation — as if taken from a great theatre of the absurd — are now publicly accessible.

Terentiev participates in the construction of Belomorkanal (the White Sea–Baltic ship canal opened in 1933), where he writes the following verses:

KREMLIN, DO YOU SEE THE DOT BELOW?
THAT'S ME PUSHING A CART,
THE SOIL OF SOCIALISM.

He was released before the end of his sentence, in 1934. Terentiev would return to Moscow, again searching unsuccessfully for a job in a theatre.

 Terentiev, a man who walked vertically

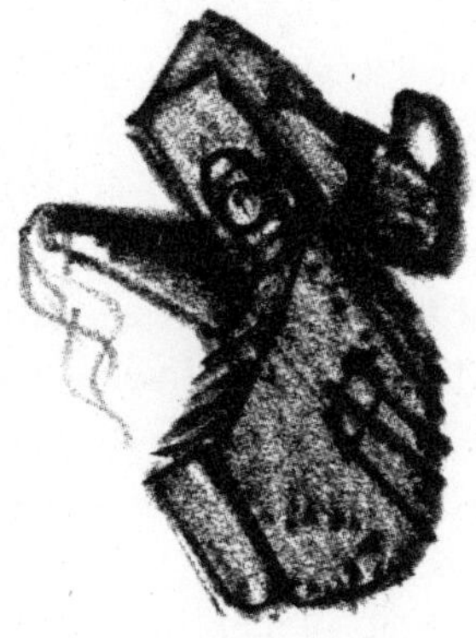

Ilya Zdanevich an angel of compact stature and an insolent singer.

 Terentiev, a man who walked vertically

As a part of the agit-brigade (photographed by Rodchenko), he voluntarily participated in the construction of the Moscow-Volga Canal, with a "guest appearance" by Maxim Gorky.

On May 28th 1937, Terentiev was arrested for the second time. He was shot dead in Butyrka prison 20 days later, seven years ahead of his own prediction.

    Terentiev, a man who walked vertically